PARENT POWER

How to Raise a Reading Superstar

by Caroline Brewer

ISBN: 978-1-7342909-8-1

Printed in the United States of America
Published by Caroline Brewer
Unchained Spirit Enterprises Publishing and Education Consulting
Washington, D.C.

Layout and cover design: Angie Steward

Cover: Isaiah, Indigo, and Roman Daniels (l-r)
spend time reading with their father, Jamie Daniels.

www.carolinebrewerbooks.com
Email: caroline@carolinebrewerbooks.com
www.Twitter.com/BrewerCaroline
www.Facebook.com/BrewerCaroline
www.Instagram.com/CarolineBrewerBooks

PARENT POWER

How to Raise a Reading Superstar

Dedication

This book is dedicated to everybody who has ever wanted to help a child learn to read.

Acknowledgments

I want to thank all of the children, teachers, and parents who have allowed me to come into their lives and share what I have learned about the power of reading, writing, and books.

I, especially, want to thank Ivory Robinson, and his mom, Terina Davis, and Elizabeth, Jasmine and their parents, Theresa and Eddie. Because you opened your hearts and homes to me, thousands more children are learning to read and to enjoy every moment of it!

What Parents are Saying

"The *Parent Power* strategies we have learned have been very valuable. We use...word games, positive reinforcement, love and patience. The genuine concern that Caroline has for children to succeed has helped instill in Jaylen the importance of reading. She teaches the importance of reading in a loving, caring, and fun way. I am truly grateful that she has come into our lives."

– Roxanne M. Carter, Washington, D.C.

"When you came to my home, you helped my special needs daughter show an interest in reading that was not there at first. She was in the 4th grade and could not read. You used her love for drawing to get her to read... you gave your time and love for what you do. God bless!"

– Theresa M. Davis, Washington, D.C.

"This book is great!!! My wife and I used the reading strategies to help our daughter with her reading. It was our hope that this book would be a tool that we could use to build her confidence, and it did just that. We watched her go from not wanting to read to looking forward to her daily reading time. She's truly developed a love for reading, and it is our hope that this would be a springboard to a love for education. Thanks, Caroline, for this great resource."

– Curtis Head, father of Cara Head, 2nd grader

"When I finished reading this book, I simply said, "WOW." This is a powerful tool that every parent and teacher should read. Rarely have I read a book that I am in 100% agreement with...(E)very suggestion made was followed with an example and directions for practical application."

– Kimmoly Rice-Ogletree,
Past PTA President and mother of two, Baltimore, MD

Table of Contents

Congratulations! By picking up this book, you've taken a major step toward helping children in your life become great readers. I promise that this is going to be one of the most amazing and memorable experiences you will ever have. And I promise that you're going to succeed as long as you live and breathe this chapter, *A Higher Way*. This book has 13 remedies but not a single method in this book or any other book will help your child become a *superstar* reader without the infusion of love and patience into every aspect of your experience.

That's the essence of the *Higher Way* and that's where our journey must start.

It is essential that you promise yourself and your child that the reading experience will be full of love, patience, and joy. Reading to a child lovingly and

patiently, to quote the old movie, *Love Story*, means never having to say you're sorry. That's our standard.

If you do have to apologize, and you probably will, it will be okay as long as you mean it and don't repeat the mistake.

Reading lovingly and patiently means allowing children to stumble, to mispronounce words, to get distracted, and act silly by making funny voices, playing with their hair, clothes, or other items, without being critical.

Reading lovingly and patiently means that you seek, always, to understand the child. Put yourself in their shoes. Empathize. For children who have not yet grasped how to read, learning is often painful. Understand that they are suffering almost every moment they sit with you and a book, magazine, news article, or some other text. Your extraordinary display of love and patience will ease that suffering, bit by bit, and slowly turn it to joy. Joy is critical to children's success, the development of confidence, and their trust in you and themselves.

If we create a great reader who's miserable when it's time to read, we have failed. Because failure is not an option, we must, must, must stay on the love and patience track. Swallow our tongues. Sit on our hands. Breathe. And smile – smile a lot.

Whatever it takes to let love and patience pour forth like the morning sun when inside we are a bit rattled, irritated, concerned, even annoyed, we must do it.

When Jared is doing what he often does – not paying attention, not listening, squirming, yawning, drumming his fingers on the table, or his head, rapping, tapping, humming, we must be patient.

When Kayla is doing what she often does – playing with items on the table, twisting her hair, making sucking sounds, digging her fingers into the sofa, air-writing, scratching incessantly, we must be understanding.

When our children cry, stamp their feet, or angrily protest instead of reading, let your love and patience wrap around their sweet little souls like cotton candy on a paper stick. Let your response be, as Stephen Covey wisely urges, not your (the child's) way or my (the adult's) way, but a higher way.

What's the higher way? Responding in a way that allows children to easily get back on track without feeling pressured, chastised, or humiliated, and that gives them a say in how to proceed. Some of the responses you might use include: "I'm here to help...How can I help?...I need your help...

We can do this. You can do this...It's going to be fun. I promise...Would you like me to read today, and you just listen?...Would you like to draw a picture or write a story instead of reading today?...Would you like to read another book or text?"

You also could say, "Talk to me…Tell me what's going on…It seems as if something is bothering you. Would you like to talk about it? …I would love for you to read with me/work with me today…I need your help so that we can finish our reading today…Thank you for staying focused…Thank you for trusting me to help you…Thank you for working so hard to become a better reader…You're doing a great job…I enjoy our time reading…I'm proud of you."

Extreme displays of love and patience and the search for a higher way when children get off track, are what's called for here. I hope you get the picture and understand that this is all for the cause of a great and happy reader. It's for the cause of children who will always remember the kindnesses we showed during one of the most difficult times of their lives. Love and patience are the requirements every day, every time we sit down with children to read and write. We might sum it up as **SOAS**: **S**eek first to understand, **O**ffer to help, **A**sk for theirs, **S**mile. With love and patience, you and your children will succeed. I promise. Have a wonderful journey!

Reading Remedy № 1
Look at that Copycat!

You may have tangible wealth untold:
Caskets of jewels and coffers of gold.
Richer than I you can never be –
I had a (parent) who read to me.

Excerpt by Strickland Gillian

An unbelievably sad thing happened in our nation's capital during early 2000. The D.C. *City Paper* reported that a teen mother starved her infant to death. She was sent to prison for the crime, but it appears to have been an accident.

A news report said the teen had been kicked out of her mother's home. She took her infant, and her toddler, to a homeless shelter. The shelter's staff noticed the mother seemed to have learning challenges. They concluded that she was capable of reading only on a kindergarten level. They called D.C.'s child protective services. By the time a social worker arrived, the teen had left the shelter and moved in with her boyfriend, who was just a couple of years older.

Over the next few weeks, the teen struggled to take care of the infant. She was given milk formula that needed to be mixed with water. But because she could barely read, she mixed in too much water. Day after day, she fed her infant milk that was so weak it hardly had nutrients. Within weeks, the baby was dead.

This might sound like an extreme case of what can happen when children grow up without learning to read well. However, during many school visits, I have met hundreds of older children who read on a low elementary level.

All of these children will not get older, have children, and starve them to death. Yet, it's clear that if some type of sustained, urgent action isn't taken to help them become self-sufficient readers, they are likely to have more trouble socially, emotionally, physically, and economically. There is no reason these challenges should continue.

We know that the ability to read well is the foundation of educational success. We also know that reading well and enjoying reading helps us grow and develop more fully, in ways that can't be measured on a test. Sadly, a large percentage of Americans has lost the habit of reading for pleasure.

In *The Read Aloud Handbook*, author Jim Trelease reports these amazing findings: "In the late 1990s, a scholarship committee interviewed the top three students in every state for a $60,000 scholarship. Only one student out of 150 had read a book for pleasure in the past year...The average 5th grader spends only 1 percent of his time with a book...Most American homes have more movies than books," even though books generally cost less. And he says, "Some lower-income homes have more TV sets than books."

If this was the case more than 20 years ago, we can only imagine how much worse the situation is now. Poor reading skills lead to low self-esteem, and low self-esteem can lead to so many other problems for children. The Nation's Report Card, which gauges reading achievement for 4th and 8th graders, in 2019 indicated that two-thirds of our students don't read on grade level. That's a big number! One of the most effective ways to get children interested in and excited about reading is for adults to read enjoyable books, newspaper and magazine articles, comics, plays, and poetry to and with them – often. Research from organizations such as the National Institute for Literacy back this up. Parents, youth leaders, and community members must find time each day to read to children and teens.

Why? Consider what my mother likes to say: "I can show you better than I can tell you." Children demonstrate this as well.

Usually, though, we're not paying attention.

Take my great niece for example. Often I would see her and say, "Good morning, darling," or "How are you, darling?"

I took for granted that she understood what I meant. One day I found out differently. Tykara, aged 4, handed me an item I had asked her to bring. "Thank you, darling!" I replied. Tykara froze with a puzzled look on her face. "Why you always call me daaar-ling?" she asked sweetly.

Caught off-guard, I, at first, laughed. "Because… darling means I love you," I answered finally, "and you're my sweetheart, and I think you're a nice little girl."

Tykara simply replied, "Oh," then skipped out of the room.

I didn't think any more of our little exchange. The next morning, I helped Tykara dress for church. I handed her her black patent leather shoes. With the biggest grin, she responded, "Thank you, darling!"

Duuuh! Tykara showed me what I already knew. Children are copycats. They watch and record much of what we say and do. When we least expect it, they play back the tape. Often, we're proud of what we see on that tape. But if we haven't been paying attention to our words and actions, that recording might make us wanna holler. The good news is that anybody can use a child's natural tendency to be a copycat to make a great reader out of the child.

Trelease says imitation is the *first and most* important way children learn. He pointed out in the late 1970s that more 5-year-olds could recite "Two all-beef patties, special sauce, lettuce, cheese, pickles, onions on a sesame seed bun," than could recite their addresses and phone numbers. Why? Because McDonald's is expert at making commercials with messages that stick like glue.

So we must keep asking ourselves what kind of commercial are we in the lives of children around us.

Research suggests that books – even elementary-aged picture books – have more difficult vocabulary than many TV programs. Books help build, strengthen, and lengthen a child's attention span. TV and video games can interfere with attention spans. The more you read to and with children, the more they'll get the message that books are important and fun.

If you want your youngsters to love books, then you must demonstrate that you love books. You must spend time lovingly and patiently reading to and with them every day. If you just can't do every day, please try every other day, or even once a week for starters. Just know that the more consistent you are, the more consistent your child will be.

When you show children, of all ages, that reading is a good and desirable thing, they will get the message, just as Tykara – my precious little copycat – demonstrated that she understood "daaar-ling" to be a term of endearment.

Reading Remedy Nº· 2
A Million Reasons to Read

Every time I ask children why it's important to read, they never fail to impress me. They answer, "Because it's fun...Because you learn a lot of words...Because you can go on a journey...Because it's something to do when you're bored..."

I smile. My heart warms. "They get it! They do get it!" my mind repeats. I then confirm to the children that, yes, all of their responses are excellent reasons to read. I tell them I'd like to share more reasons with them, if they don't mind. And, of course, they don't.

First, I explain how reading is related to snowflakes. Softly a snowflake falls from the sky to the ground. As you watch it dance, a twinkle appears in your eyes and a little smile creases your face. But then, if the snow begins to fall faster, and develops into a blizzard, your smile starts to turn into concern – especially if you're at school and didn't remember to bring your hat, mittens, or boots. A few snowflakes here and there won't hurt anybody. A blizzard – is another story. So it goes with books. Having one book fall into our lives every now and then doesn't change anything. If we get a blizzard of books into our lives, though, that's going to make a difference. That's what we want children to have and read – a blizzard's worth of books.

Why? Because books are the gifts that pay us back. I ask children if they had a choice between $5 and a book, which would they choose. Most answer honestly. They would choose the money. I don't judge, and reply that that's fine. It's their choice. I then ask the few who said they would choose the book to explain why. Without fail, they tell their classmates exactly what I am thinking and know to be true: $5 really doesn't buy a whole lot. It might buy school lunch for a day or two, or a burger and fries at a fast-food joint. After the food is eaten and the money is spent, you'll never benefit from it again. Not so with a book. Books are forever.

Cover of *Kara Finds Sunshine on a Rainy Day*, illustrated by Harlem School of the Arts students

I follow up by telling them about the joys of reading many books that have made me a wiser, kinder, more patient and thoughtful person. I also have met many children and adults who have told me how much my books meant to them.

A 12-year-old boy, who was one of the first children to read *Kara Finds Sunshine on a Rainy Day*, sent me a thank-you card that in part read, "Thank you, Caroline and friends. You guys changed my life around." *Kara Finds Sunshine* is a book about hope and healing that I wrote shortly after 9/11. People of all ages, facing all kinds of challenges, relate to its message of finding hope in difficult times.

This 12-year-old lived in a New Jersey home for abused and neglected children. He was terribly upset about being separated from his mother. He would rarely speak and had not made any friends. I found out later that she was an immigrant with seven other children. I was told that she had no job and had a hard time making ends meet but was neither abusive nor neglectful. The local AKA sorority bought books for this boy and 54 other children at the group home. I came during their monthly birthday party celebration, read *Kara Finds Sunshine*, and gave out cookies with the book.

A week after my visit, a counselor called to tell me that after my visit, the boy became a new person. He opened up, she said, "like a flower," began speaking and smiling more often and making friends. After I received the boy's thank-you card, I volunteered to be his mentor – which, of course, was more rewarding for both of us than $5.

I wrote a poem about reasons to read. It's called *Why I Read*. It's meant to be read aloud with lots of energy and enthusiasm initially by the adult, with children announcing the words in bold, until they can read the poem on their own. Before reading, though, discuss with your children the reasons why you like to read and ask them for theirs. Afterwards, compare your reasons and the children's to the poem's. *Enjoy!*

Why I Read

by Author Caroline Brewer © 2019

I read because it's an adventurous thing.
I hug a book like it's a **DIAMOND RING**.
I read lyrics that make me want to **SING!**
And fly real high with my literary **WINGS.**

Sometimes I read like **CRAZY**.
Can't call us readers **LAZY**.
Sometimes I read real **FAST,**
Sometimes, though, I read **SLOW,**
to make the **STORY LAAAST**!

When I open a book, **I OPEN A DOOR**
to destinations both near and far away –
EXOTIC, mountainous, tranquil, bustling,
at least that's what the authors say.
I take their word for it, 'cause they know how to make
MY IMAGINATION come out **TO PLAY.**

When I open a book, I see **DEAD PEOPLE**,
and alive ones too! They're driving fast cars, gazing at stars,
and **DOING THE BOOGALOO!**

I read to answer questions that shatter **MY SLEEP**.
Reading dissolves puzzles for me that run **DEEP-SEA DEEP.**
I read with the excitement of summer and **SPRING**.
I read 'cause ain't nothing better I can do for this **BRAIN!**
I read with hope that for better
our world will soon **CHANGE!**
I read myself right into the magic of my lifelong **DREAMS!**

I read because it gives me information that I don't know.
I read **LANGSTON HUGHES' POETRY**
'cause **THE BROTHER'S GOT FLOW.**

I read to find **THE LIGHT!**
Sometimes it's out of **MY SIGHT!**
I read when **IT'S HARD!**
I got books by **THE YARD!**
I read when it's silent,
Just me **BY MYSELF.**
I read by accident, you know,
just like **EVERYBODY ELSE!**

I will **NEVER** stop reading,
no matter the struggle or strife.
See, my ancestors hardly got the chance.
So **THAT'S INSPIRATION** for the rest of my life.

Nobody will cut my ears if they **SEE ME WITH A BOOK,**
Or slice my back **WITH WHIPS** that bend me to shame.
Reading helps me shape **MY FUTURE** and boldly reclaim
our people's **PROUD HISTORY.**
We are no longer in **CHAINS!**

So wipe your weeping eyes.
I read because **MAYA ANGELOU** told us
we've got reason to **RISE.**
I **RISE** and I read because reading **SETS ME FREE**
and free I plan to stay.
So if you don't like my reading, friend,
ADIOS, and **BONNE JOURNEE.**

Reading Remedy №. 3
Repeat after Me and Set that Superstar Reader Free

Repetition and echo-reading are some of the fastest ways to increase a child's reading ability. Echo-reading is reading just a word, phrase, or sentence in a text and having the child repeat or "echo" it back to you. It's fun, it keeps children alert during the reading experience, and helps build their vocabulary and fluency.

Repetition is simply having children read the same text or sections of a text over and over, with guidance. Doing so will build fluency and mastery. The National Institute For Literacy concluded this in a 2003 study. Fluency is when a child can read smoothly, without pausing and stumbling over numerous words. A fluent reader is not just a faster reader. A fluent reader is a reader who can read quickly and smoothly and who understands most of what he reads.

You can check your child's comprehension by asking him to explain certain sentences, paragraphs, pages, or sections of text. When a child's comprehension increases, his overall reading ability increases. Not to mention the joy he experiences.

In addition, when a child becomes a more fluent reader, he becomes a more confident reader. As a confident reader, he's going to get more involved in school and will more likely do his homework – because he now understands the assignments. Getting more involved in school and completing homework assignments will help him improve in other subjects.

In 2004, I began tutoring an Indiana boy named Ivory. Ivory had just finished 5th grade. His mother told me his teacher said he read on a 2nd grade level. It could have been lower. Ivory was not a fluent reader and couldn't pronounce a long list of words that had just one syllable, such as hide, seek, show, done, and keep. He did not understand or remember very much of what he read.

Parent Power   How to Raise a Reading Superstar   Caroline Brewer

I read lovingly and patiently with Ivory once a week for about 90 minutes. Before beginning a book with this charming young man, I would ask him to read the book (always a 32-page children's picture book) or a chapter from a book to me. I would time him. Next, I would read the entire book or chapter to Ivory and ask him to follow along as I read. The third time through, I would read a page or a paragraph to Ivory, then ask him to echo or repeat what I had read. The fourth and final time through, Ivory would read the entire book or chapter on his own.

Repeatedly, Ivory would at least double his reading speed by the final read-through. For instance, it took him 45 minutes to read for the first time *Kara Finds Sunshine on a Rainy Day*. At the end our session, Ivory read Kara in less than 20 minutes.

After that fourth read, I would ask him questions about the story or chapter to see how much of it he understood. Ivory demonstrated that he had a much deeper understanding of what the story was about by the fourth time than he had the first time. As a result, Ivory's confidence grew. I could see his shoulders rise and his face loosen as he read. He would smile in between sections and glance at me to make sure that he was reading well.

He knew how hard he was working to get through each book or chapter.

In its Repetition report, the NIFL also urged that: "Students should read and reread until a certain level

of fluency is reached...usually four times is sufficient."
In *Partnering for Fluency*, Mary Kay Moskal and Camille
Blachowicz write that repetition or repeated reading
is "decidedly one of the best strategies for fluency
development." The authors also found that repetition
provides adults with a great way to test how well a
child is reading.

After a month or so, I quit timing Ivory before
reading to him. I simply read the text to him first.
Many children with poor reading skills might become

frustrated having to read an unfamiliar text by themselves. I now recommend the adult or older sibling read the text first so that the child has a smoother introduction to it. It's so important for struggling readers to enjoy their experiences with books. If a child is pushed too fast or if an adult doesn't recognize his frustration, he is likely to stop trying. Many of us would do the same.

I encourage you to develop a reading routine that includes at least three readings of the same text using repetition and echo-reading.

In January of Ivory's sixth grade year, six months after we began working together, I gave him a reading test used by all the district's 6th grade teachers. He tested at a 4.4 grade reading level. Interestingly enough, the two questions he missed, that would have put him at 4.7 grade level, were questions with answers that I might have missed because they were not constructed well. The questions could have easily confused any reader at any grade level.

Two things are important to note about this major increase in reading level. The first is that during Ivory's first three months of tutoring, he received no additional reading help from his family, as this program requires. I'll explain later how we overcame that challenge. The second issue to note is that I forgot to closely examine the test or go over test-taking strategies with Ivory before giving him the test. I believed then, and think his progress in recent years has shown, that he was reading at a higher grade level than at what he tested. (It should be noted also that Ivory raised his Language Arts grade from a low C to a solid B during our 6 months together.)

If I had given this child the same kind of instruction before the test that he would have received from a classroom teacher, I know his performance would have been even better. There were many questions on the test that made me do a double take and read the essay more closely before choosing an answer. If this happened to me, I know that it happened to Ivory, as well as it does to many of our children who experience fear and anxiety when confronted with yet another so-called test of intelligence.

I'm happy to report that two years after the tutoring ended, Ivory was still making progress in reading. I contacted his mother in May 2007, just before he finished 8th grade. She told me he had earned an A in Language Arts. I contacted the district and got confirmation of that fact from Ivory's middle school principal, who, in a few days, was going to preside over the year-end awards ceremony where Ivory would receive Language Arts honors. All of this from a child who was reading somewhere between a first and second grade level just before the start of sixth grade. I can tell you that the loving and patient relationship I established with Ivory, along with consistent read-alouds that involved repetition and echo-reading, worked long-lasting magic in his life.

Reading Remedy № 4
Rhymes are a Superpower that Build Literacy Hour by Hour

What do Jay-Z, Mother Goose, Salt-N-Pepa, and Dr. Seuss have in common? Most students can tell you. They are rhyme masters and have used this wonderful tool to become rich and/or famous. Mother Goose is just a character to whom hundreds of nursery rhymes are credited. Still, her collection of rhymes captivates us from infancy and holds sway until the grave. Nursery rhymes have been a category on the popular TV show *Jeopardy!* We never, ever forget those nursery rhymes. Nor do we forget the magical and innocent images of childhood that they help us recall.

This is why rhymes and rhyming books are excellent tools for helping emerging readers, of all ages, increase their skills instantly and for the long term.

Literacy experts tell us that rhymes build memory, vocabulary, and confidence *faster than any other reading technique*. Confidence is crucial in helping struggling readers see themselves as fluent, successful readers.

Read-Aloud Guru Jim Trelease advises, "Rhymes are the closest things to a mother's heartbeat. They are comfortable and predictable." No wonder children love them! Rhymes, of course, are introduced to children at infancy and help them take their first steps up the rungs of literacy achievement. After listening to nursery rhymes during toddler and pre-school years, rhymes are key to the next huge step in language acquisition as children learn the alphabet. Rhymes and songs make it easier for children to understand letter sounds, hear all the words, understand how words are put together, how to speak and read with emotion, how to be better writers and spellers, and how to recall words and ideas.

Researchers say that a solid reading foundation includes children mastering at least eight nursery rhymes by first grade. Use the list at the end of this chapter to build that solid foundation for the children in your life.

Importantly, rhymes are fun. When children enjoy reading and being read to, they are more likely to want to read on their own. Rhymes also are a highly effective way to teach difficult concepts across the curriculum. They provide educators with unlimited opportunities to boost a child's achievement level.

In 2006, I spoke to Raymond Mark, then high school math department chair at a school outside New York City. Raymond sings the quadratic formula to the tune of *Pop Goes the Weasel* and *Row, Row, Row Your Boat* to his Algebra II students. The formula is used to calculate such things as the precise timing of missiles and rocket launches. Having an easy way to remember the formula is a gift. Raymond's students absolutely love and are grateful for it! But many of his colleagues are too "embarrassed" to share the rhyming formula with their students. Imagine how many more students, especially in low-performing high schools, we could entice to take high-level math classes if they knew that complex formulas could be easily digested with rhyming schemes.

Speaking of rhymes for young children, older children will master reading with the use of songs and raps. Simply print out their favorites, looking for the

rhyming patterns, sing them as often as they like, and then ask them to read the songs/raps. Encourage them to write new versions of their favorite songs and raps or draft their own. Some examples of raps I've written are below and you'll find out more about helping children use writing to improve as readers and writers and speakers in the chapter on writing in this book.

Remember nimble Jack? "Jack be nimble, Jack be quick, Jack jump over the candlestick." Let's learn from Jack's skill in getting children over obstacles. Use rhymes to be nimble. Use rhymes to be quick. Rhymes boost reading and writing. Anybody can master this trick!

Seven Superpowers of Rhyme

1. Children become better readers.
2. Children become better writers.
3. Children become better spellers.
4. Children understand and identify letter sounds and parts of words more easily.
5. Children build vocabulary faster.
6. Children improve their recall of words and story concepts.
7. Children read and speak with emotion - with inflection – and pronounce words in ways that are exciting and interesting and that create imagery and emotion.

Three Popular Forms of Rhyme
that will help older children improve
reading and writing skills:

(Couplets, Limericks, and Songs/Raps)

Couplet - Two lines of verse which rhyme and form a unit alone or as part of a poem.

Two examples of couplets from *Kara Finds Sunshine on a Rainy Day:*

One summer morning, little Kara woke up.
She smelled her mom cooking a breakfast of
pancakes and syrup.

The sun shines day and night.
It spreads its rays from the highest heights.

Two examples of couplets in *Barack Obama: A Hip Hop Tale of King's Dream Come True:*

Gather around children, have you heard?
I have a dream to share, in rhyming words.

My dream begins on Chicago's South side,
during hot summer days and cold winter nights.

A man named Barack Obama walked the streets,
paying careful attention to the people he would meet.

One example of a couplet from *Darius Daniels: Game On!:*

Now I can read a book all by myself.
I don't need help from nobody else.

Limerick - A five-line poem with a notable rhythm that sometimes ends with a surprising twist. The first, second and fifth lines, the longer lines, rhyme. The third and fourth shorter lines rhyme. (A-A-B-B-A).

Example of a limerick from *Darius Daniels: Game On!:*

D changed his smile to a frown
Pushed his head all the way down
Wondering if through the whipped cream
held the calm of the sweetest dreams
or enough nightmares for a whole town.

Example of a limerick from Poet Edward Lear:

There was an old man in a tree,
Whose whiskers were lovely to see;
*   But the birds of the air,*
*   Pluck'd them perfectly bare,*
To make themselves nests on that tree.

Songs and Raps

Below is a pronoun rap I wrote and taught 6th grade students. They learned the definition and aced a test on pronouns in a matter of minutes:

The Pronoun Rap by Caroline Brewer ©2008

"A noun is a person, place, or thing, like teacher, city, street, or a diamond ring.

Pronouns take the place of a noun, like she or he sitting in for a clown.

A pronoun by itself doesn't tell you a thing. 'It' could be a car, a house, or a diamond ring."

One example of a rap from *Darius Daniels: Game On!:*

First verse (in the book)

I love books like kids love candy.
I love books like beaches love sandy.
I love books like corn loves to pop.
I love books like hip loves to hop.

Second verse (used with live audiences)

I love books like icing loves cake.
I love books like pies love to bake.
I love books like cars love to drive.
I love books like bees love the hive.

Example of a rap in *Barack Obama: A Hip Hop Tale of King's Dream Come True:*

> *People are people, no matter their skin.*
> *The real you is the person that lives within.*

9 Nursery Rhymes Children Should Know
by 1st Grade for a Solid Reading Foundation

Compiled and revised by
Author Caroline Brewer © 2020

Hey, Diddle, Diddle
(Revised by Caroline Brewer ©2020)

Hey diddle diddle,
The cat played the fiddle,
The cow jumped over the moon.
The little dog laughed to see so many jokes,
And the dish mirror-danced with the spoon.

Itsy-Bitsy Spider

The itsy-bitsy spider
Climbed up the water spout.
Down came the rain
And washed the spider out.
Out came the sun
And dried up all the rain,
So the itsy-bitsy spider
Climbed up the spout again!

Little Miss Muffet (Rap)
(Revised by Caroline Brewer ©2020)

> *Little Miss Muffet sat on a tuffet,*
> *Eating her PB & J.*
> *Along came a spider.*
> *He sat down beside her,*
> *And then they began to play.*
> *(Hey, hey!)*

> *(Spiders control insects, without spiders, we would face famine)*

Mary had a Little Lamb

> *Mary had a little lamb,*
> *Its fleece was white as snow.*
> *And ev'ry where that Mary went,*
> *The lamb was sure to go.*

> *It followed her to school one day,*
> *Which was against the rule.*
> *It made the children laugh and play,*
> *To see a lamb at school.*

Row, Row, Row Your Boat

> *Row, row, row your boat*
> *Gently down the stream.*
> *Merrily, merrily, merrily, merrily,*
> *Life is but a dream.*

Wheels on the Bus

The wheels on the bus go round and round,
Round and round,
Round and round.
The wheels on the bus go round and round,
All through the town.

Jack is Cool
(Revised by Caroline Brewer ©2020)

Jack is cool;
Jack is quick.
Jack hops over
the pile of sticks.

Humpty Jumpty
(Revised by Caroline Brewer ©2020)

Humpty Jumpty
danced on a wall.
Humpty Jumpty
never did fall.

All the king's horses,
and all the king's men
praised Humpty Jumpty
again and again!

Sherry Had a Canary
(Revised by Caroline Brewer ©2020)

Sherry had a tiny bird,
Feathers bright and yellow;
Skinny legs, and I tell you this,
He was a handsome fellow.

The sweetest notes the bird did sing,
And happy that made Sherry:
Near the cage, she'd always sit,
To hear her own canary.

Reading Remedy № 5
30 Minutes a Day Chases Reading Blues Away

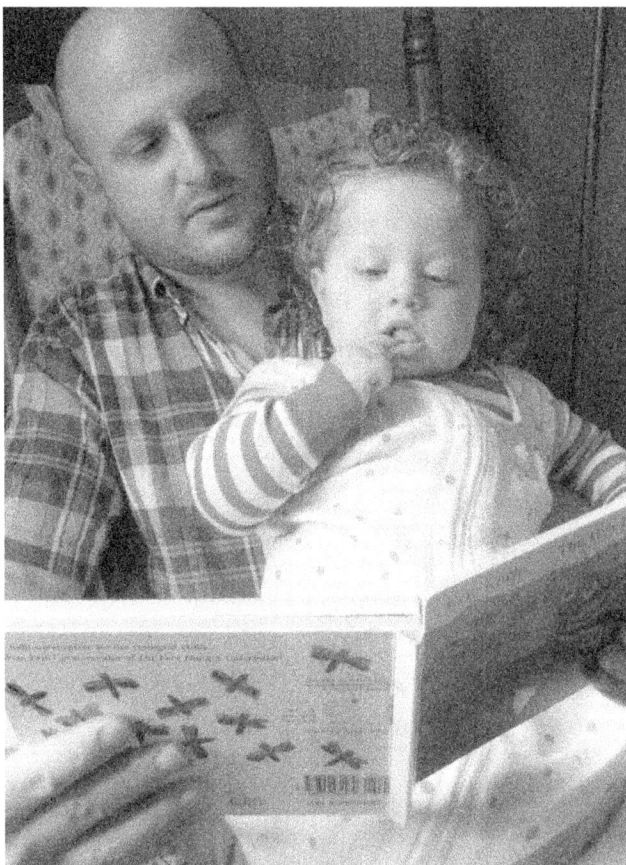

Lovingly, patiently, and excitedly read to and with your child at least 30 minutes each day.

There are some reading programs and experts who suggest reading aloud for at least 15 or 20 minutes a day. Others suggest 30. I recommend 30 because it's what the U.S. Department of Education recommends from infancy, and I find it to be the minimum a child needs to make up for what I call the "lost years," described in a study that I'll share more about below and in other chapters.

The U.S. Department of Education says, "Reading to a child for 30 minutes per day from infancy helps prepare a child to learn. A 5-year-old who has not been read to daily will enter kindergarten with far fewer hours of 'literacy nutrition' than a child who has been read to daily from infancy."

What the Department of Education is saying, in effect, is that when you're reading to children, you're feeding children – feeding them the literacy nutrition that will help them grow and blossom as learners. This is where *Parent Power* comes in. Parents, guardians, reaching coaches, tutors, and community members who commit to reading to a child lovingly and patiently, every day, for at least 30 minutes are the answers to the gaps in literacy nutrition.

Pediatrician Robert E. Burke puts the importance of reading to children daily this way in an online article for the Scott & White Healthcare Community: "During those first few years, you're developing the capacity to learn. The brain is kind of a blank slate that will be molded and developed. And reading is one of the most influential ways to accomplish that."

He added, "If you could give kids something that would prevent school failure and that would prevent a lot of behavioral problems, you'd want to give it to everybody," he said. "So, in order to be successful in school, you have to be able to read."

The best dose of this "medicine" to prevent school failure and behavioral problems is to read to them for at least 30 minutes a day.

All of the children I tutored, including Ivory, were asked to read 30 minutes each day in between our sessions. And when they did, they experienced tremendous gains that helped them close the gap created by the lost years when they were not receiving such a rich diet of words.

In addition to reading with love and patience for 30 minutes, you will do the children in your life a huge favor if you read with excitement and drama! Letting your inner drama queens and kings run wild is another fantastic way to boost literacy nutrition and create joyful memories from reading.

Annie Murphy Paul, author of *The Brilliant Blog*, once wrote that "The research of Arthur Glenberg, a professor of psychology at Arizona State University, has demonstrated that when children are given the opportunity to act out a written text, their reading comprehension can actually ***double.***"

Imagine that! By sounding out the sounds - such as raising your voice, squealing, laughing loudly or in a silly way, speaking in a whisper, singing! and moving your hands and other body parts to mimic the movements of characters in the story, such as beating on a table, running in place, waving wildly as if you're trying to get someone's attention – you can double how much children understand as you're reading the story. This is priceless, not only because of the power it gives you as a parent. It's priceless because it's a tool that costs nothing except your imagination and your willingness to go all in to make your child a reading superstar.

And once children start to gain confidence and skill as readers, they can call on their inner drama queens and kings as they read. You'll be thrilled at how much fun reading becomes.

So, how does a busy parent or adult like you find time to read to and with children 30 minutes every single day? You don't find it. **You make it.**

Think about the best time of day when there are the fewest distractions or chances for interruptions and make that your dedicated time for reading. I recommend setting this time at least a couple hours prior to bedtime so that you and your child are more alert. In addition to your dedicated time, you can have your child read to you while you're driving, or you're both traveling by bus, subway, or taxi. You also can squeeze in some of those 30 minutes while you're waiting for health or dental care appointments.

Keep books, magazines, or newspapers with you at all times, so that whenever there is a spare moment, you can use it to read to and with your child or have your child read to you. Encourage children to keep reading materials with them as well.

However, I recognize there will be some days when you just can't squeeze in those 30 minutes. Perhaps you are a parent who works two jobs, or weekends, or night shifts. Perhaps you are a parent whose job requires that you travel. Whatever makes it difficult for you to read in person, consider finding a trusted adult, siblings, or relative to read with your child when you can't be available.

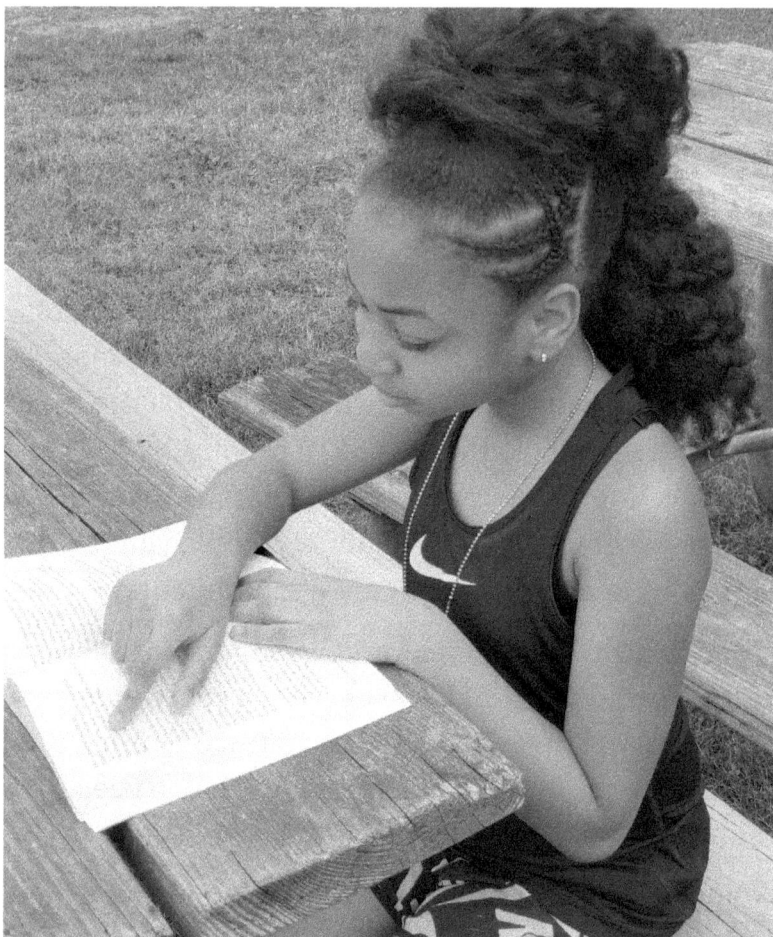

Another great way to keep your child reading daily with great guidance is to use audiobooks that you buy, borrow or exchange, or get from the library. Children can play the audio download and read along to it with their digital or printed copy of the book. Having a parent or loving adult by a child's side is the best way for children to fall in love with books and reading.

But for those days when parents can't sit down with children, let them read with a recorded version of the book.

If you have a voice recorder – voice recorders and video recorders are on all cell phones and most tablets – record yourself reading a story or text for your child and let them listen to it when you're not available, or for extra practice. You can also use video conferencing apps, such as Zoom, Google Meets, Free Conference Call, and Facebook's Messenger Video.

After three months of tutoring and not seeing as much progress as I knew he was capable of, I realized that his lack of daily practice with an older sibling or adult was not only slowing his progress, but it was upsetting him emotionally. On several occasions as he struggled to read, he would get so frustrated he would cry. I realized that we needed to do something different. I began taping all the stories and chapters we read each week.

He listened to them and read along with them for 30 minutes each day. We both recognized that this small addition to our routine resulted in a huge and almost instant boost to his reading skill and confidence.

There is no substitute for having a parent or caring adult lovingly, patiently, and excitedly read to a child each day, but giving a child a recorded version of a story or text is a meaningful way to speed and maintain progress and give the adult a break when it's needed. It also can be fun for both. As children improve their reading ability, they might want to hear recordings of themselves reading, so taking turns reading the text and acting out the story can be a great way to engage children in the experience of reading. It gives them ownership and increases the joy of reading – which is the ultimate goal.

Reading Remedy N⁰· 6
Constant Praise Goes a Long Ways

You will recall our discussion in the opening chapter, *The Higher Way*, of how important it is to lovingly and patiently listen to children as they read. When you are working with your children, you are building your relationship with them. Never, ever criticize them. When children are learning to read and are working on improving their skills, criticizing or being impatient with them will make them want to give up. Reading is such an emotional experience, children, regardless of age, need constant encouragement.

Every effective teacher has excellent relationships with their students. The same is true for parents. It doesn't mean we do everything perfectly or never have regrets. It just means that we must always keep our eyes on the health of the relationship. The late longtime Educator Clare Cherry shared great advice about how to keep the adult-child relationship healthy when she said, "What I want for myself, I must also want for you. What I want from you, I must also be willing to give."

Another late educator, my dear friend, Professor Carol Manigault, pointed out that researchers long ago concluded that, in an overwhelmingly negative atmosphere, filled with negative expectations, it is impossible for students to perform as well as when they are treasured and considered worthwhile and valued.

We must remember that the definition of a child is "an immature being." Children are by nature immature. Silly. Unaware of how to make the best choices. That's why they need loving and mature parents and adults in their lives. At the same time, children are innocent. When they "act out," it's a cry for help and guidance. Knowing and understanding this will help us build strong, healthy, and positive relationships with them.

There is science that tells us that negative messages stick in our minds a lot longer than positive messages. In fact, I recall a study that said in effect that for the worst possible negative act a person committed, they

would have to commit 25 positive acts to limit the damage done by that ONE negative act. And this was a study done with adults. Negative acts, including words, can damage children for the rest of their lives.

I've heard stories from many adults of how the negative words they heard as children still ring in their ears and affect how they feel about themselves, the kinds of decisions they make, and their relationships with friends, families, co-workers, and children. Take a few moments to examine your own life and the words that you still hear an adult saying about you.

Once, when I was consulting in an elementary school, I heard a five-year-old boy in kindergarten breathing heavily and crying as he slowly shuffled past the teacher's lounge where I was sitting. Let's call him J.J. I had been reading *Kara Finds Sunshine on a Rainy Day* to J.J.'s class in recent days and, on the first day, he made up a song about sunshine and burst out singing in the middle of my reading. It was one of the sweetest reactions I ever recall from a group of students. I asked all the children to join in with me and sing his song. It moved me to see that he found the story so uplifting, it inspired him to sing.

But on this day, J.J. was in a stormy place. I asked him to talk to me and tell me why he was crying. He explained through his tears that he was being sent to the office because he'd gotten into a fight. When I asked why he'd gotten into a fight, he balled his tiny fists, gritted his teeth, and screamed, "Because I'm eeeee-vil!"

I was stunned. My heart ached for J.J. I assured him that he was only good and we talked about ways he could avoid getting into fights. He calmed down and headed for the principal's office. The school year was just about over at this time, and I never had the chance to see J.J. again. I think about him often, and hope and pray that somewhere along the way, someone planted enough loving and nurturing words into him to forever erase the suggestion that he was evil.

Yet, he's not the first child I've met who believed that there was nothing good about him or his life. During the 2019-2020 school year, I heard from a teacher who said one of her 4th graders was beating himself in the head and yelling that he wanted to die. Let's call him Travis. Travis had had a difficult time at home and had moved to a new school in a new city with a different parent. Early in the school year, he found himself being chastised by two different teachers on the same day. His teacher shared her story just about the time that *Darius Daniels: Game On!* was coming out. I offered to send Travis an Advance Reader's Copy (ARC) with a note inviting him to be my pen pal. She thought it was a great idea, so I sent the book.

Travis and I became pen pals. His teachers became more sensitive to his need for encouragement. The new parent he lived with was also encouraging. In a matter of days, Travis had a new attitude. He had been two grade levels behind in reading but gained so much confidence with *Darius Daniels* and the supportive atmosphere he was in that he constantly volunteered to read to his peers and excelled throughout the school year. He never again expressed a desire to die or harm himself.

Travis and J.J. are strong reminders that we have the chance each day to plant the kinds of words into children's hearts and minds that will ensure their social and emotional growth and prosperity.

No matter how many words children stumble over or mispronounce; no matter how frustrated they become, we must keep encouraging them. Phrases such as, "You can do it! I'm here to help you…Reading is like dancing, or playing an instrument, or walking. Once you feel the rhythm, everything just flows. You're not even aware of how it's happening. It just does…Lots of people in history have had trouble learning to read. But they kept trying until they succeeded…You will succeed. I am here to make sure that you do," can make all the difference.

Your encouragement is necessary during reading and writing, and it's necessary all day long, no matter the activity or experience. Trust me. Constant praise goes a long, long ways toward healing our children and keeping them strong.

Reading Remedy № 7
Ask to Find Out What the Book's About

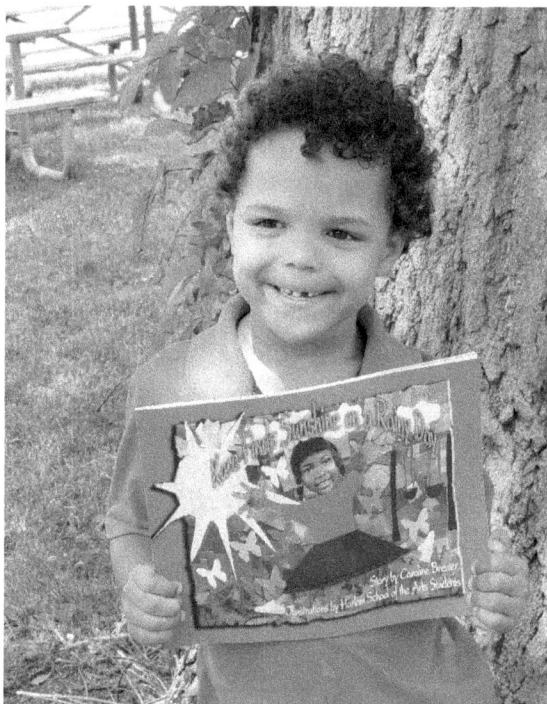

Lovingly and patiently ask children questions about each book or section of a book that you and they read. This will help you see how much of the story children understand as they read or listen to the book and it will build their confidence as they demonstrate they understand what they've read or listened to.

It's important to ask questions that are considered "open" or "open-ended." These questions are more likely to generate discussion, thoughtfulness, and be answered in complete sentences.

Questions that begin with What, Why, and How are the best open-ended questions. Since it's important to have as much fun with questions as with all other aspects of the reading experience, remember always to toss in a few easy, fun, and silly questions.

Here are sample "open" examples with a few for kicks:

"What did you find funny in this chapter?"

"Why do you think the axman was confused?"

"How did you feel when you heard Derrick was kidnapped?"

"What do you think will happen now?"

"Why do you think Juan ran into the woods?"

"How would you react if you were in that situation?"

"What did you feel when Jose fell into the hole?"

"Why do you think Tamia's mom put her on punishment?"

"How do you think the story would be different if James were rolling a giant peach, instead of a flying on a giant peach?"

"What's the silliest thing Maria did in this chapter?"

"How would you act sillier than Jared?"

"What's another way that Jennifer could show that she hated broccoli?"

When you ask these kinds of questions during the story, ask just one at a time, and keep them short so that you don't interrupt the flow of your child's reading.

You also can ask "closed" questions to check whether your child remembers key facts. Mixing some easy "closed" questions with more challenging "open" questions will also help build your child's confidence.

"Closed" questions will generate yes or no responses, or either a response that is right or wrong. They can begin with Who, What, How, Did, Do, Does, or Can.

Examples include:

"How many times did Alan try the experiment before it worked?"

"What year was the game of basketball invented?"

"Who was the 44th president?"

"How often did Alison go to the store?"

"What made Jamaria so angry on her birthday?"

"Did Crystal like going to San Diego?"

"Can LeBron fly a kite?"

"Does Kaylyn like squid?"

"Do Brad and Raymond like visiting the farm?"

The sample questions above would work well for elementary-aged children and children reading on an elementary grade level. For older children and children reading on middle school and high school grade levels, consider the examples below of "open" questions. Most are taken from *Questioning Strategies* by the Center for Teaching Excellence, University of Illinois at Urbana-Champaign.

Important note and advice also from *Questioning Strategies*: In cases of younger children, if they respond with an "incorrect or weak answer," give them credit for trying by saying something such as, "I see you're thinking…Thank you for giving that a try…How about we think about it this way?" Then offer a hint in a "follow up question that will lead them to the correct or stronger answer." For older students who respond "incorrectly with a weak answer," give them credit for trying, and "point out what's incorrect about the answer," without giving away the right answer, then offer a hint in a "follow up question that will lead them to the correct or stronger answer."

Sample questions for older students or students reading on higher grade levels might include:

"What is the most important idea you got from this chapter?"

"If you were telling your friend about what happened in this chapter or on this page, what would you say?"

"What are this character's values?"

"What are this character's beliefs?"

"How do you know that?"

"What part of the text led you to that conclusion?"

"What might happen if this practice were outlawed?"

"What would be a fun way to ridicule this law?"

"In what ways do you relate to this character's experience?"

"Do you agree with the character's boss, father, mother, grandparent?"

"Why do you think the character chose to skip school?"

"Who is the most influential person in this character's life?"

"What do you think is going to happen now that he lied?"

"What would be a fun way to punish the character without hurting her?"

Remember, children are going to grow as readers, thinkers, and learners by being able to answer open and closed questions. The better they get at answering questions, the more they will enjoy the experience. In a later chapter, you find out how to have *even more fun* with questions!

Reading Remedy № 8
A Child's Picture is Worth a Thousand Words

Lovingly and patiently work with children to draw, color, or paint a picture that reflects what they learned from, or liked most about, the story. Art is a young child's favorite language. It can be more profound in describing how children feel and think than words. For older children, art can be a more

exciting and fruitful avenue to express themselves. It can come in handy when they're upset or confused, and the right words don't easily come to mind. Keep pencils, crayons, markers, and paint within reach so that once a story has been read, children can share what they learned from a story by drawing or painting a picture that expresses their thoughts.

As an author who has published four books using children's illustrations, I promise that you will be impressed by children's art. Children have a way of telling stories through art that is very different from adults. It can be more honest and straightforward. It can be unbelievably cute. It can be touching in a way that makes you want to cry. Often, it's very funny.

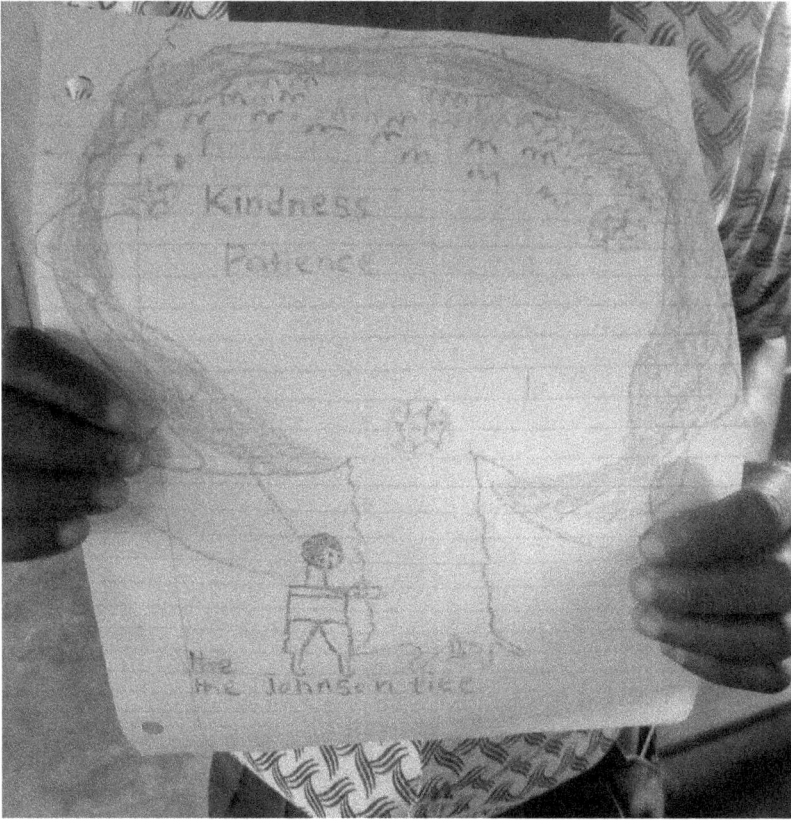

As you watch children create art based on a book or story, be careful not to criticize how they draw or the colors they use. As with reading, criticism will make them want to give up drawing and expressing themselves. It could lower their self-esteem.

Art is a way of communicating and it's important that children communicate with us in as many ways as possible. Because children are immature by virtue of age and experience, they don't have the vocabulary or life experience to verbally discuss especially difficult or complicated ideas. But art is a way for them to share

what they're thinking and feeling about difficult and complicated situations. Trust me, if you look closely and have patient and thoughtful talks about the art, you'll find it to be revealing and helpful.

In the Hurricane Katrina edition of *Kara Finds Sunshine on a Rainy Day*, I recall being wowed by the artwork of a 5-year-old. She had illustrated the vignette about Harriet Tubman. It was full of green – watercolor green hues and magazine pictures of grassy areas and forests. This, it turns out, was the key to Harriet's ability to be such a successful Underground Railroad conductor. From a very young age, Harriet's father had taught her to become familiar with the woods and how to navigate it fearlessly. I did not have a discussion on this level with the 5-year-old artist. I don't know that her teachers did, either. Whatever the case, with just the six lines in the story that described Harriet's heroism in leading the enslaved to freedom, this child got the idea that connection to nature was essentially a part of Harriet's DNA. A 5-year-old communicated this big idea that had yet to be explored in books with watercolors, glue, and portions of magazine pages. I remain deeply impressed.

Another child, who was just 7, drew an illustration about Kim Phuc, who as a 9-year-old girl was burned by napalm (and almost died) during the Vietnam War. This boy created a moving and emotional portrait, with a mixture of dark and vibrant colors, giving off the sense of fire, smoke, and bright morning skies, dotted with the heads of bald female dolls. Many of those who died from the bombings suffered burns over their bodies, including their heads. Again, I never had a discussion on this level with the children or this artist, and even if his teachers did, he produced a piece of art with depth that would seem beyond the reach of a child his age.

All this to say, if you let children draw and paint in response to stories, they're going to tell you something that they might not otherwise be able to communicate, and you'll be so glad they did.

So, once children finish their pictures, congratulate them, and ask them to tell you about the work. It's okay if you don't understand all of it. They are creating art from their world. As long as they are pleased with it, that's all that matters. They need to know that they are always going to be safe and welcomed in sharing. If they try to compare their work to another child, let them know that they should not do that. The way children choose to tell their story is special because it comes from them. Their work should not look like anybody else's because each child is unique and perfect as they are.

Reading Remedy № 9

Books They Write
Will Send Them to Higher Heights

The verdict is in. If you want to grow good readers, you have to nurture their writing skills. The 2010 report *Writing to Read* by the Carnegie Corporation found that writing improves student comprehension, engagement, thoughtfulness, and, among other things, their ability to read fluently and accurately.

So, dear readers, I strongly recommend that you lovingly and patiently work with your children to help them write and illustrate books or essays, at least twice a month. How do we get them to write – and enjoy it? Excellent question! The same way we get them to read. We invite them into the process. We make it exciting and relevant. And we explain that writing is as simple as talking on paper. As they think about writing, invite them to imagine that they are talking to a family member or friend. As they effortlessly (or not) start saying what they would tell you, a brother, or friend, encourage them to tell it to the paper.

"I don't want to write." Tell that to the paper. "I think this is dumb." Talk to the paper. "I don't know nothing about Egypt." Great! The paper needs to hear that! Over and over, I've seen the most resistant children – from elementary to high school, whether diagnosed with learning disabilities or gripped by fear – start writing.

My experience with Elizabeth, a brilliant 4th grader I had the pleasure to tutor, gives some clues as to how you might start.

Elizabeth had just finished third grade when I met her. She had been in Special Education classes all of her life. School reports said she had made little progress in any subject. When I tried to test Elizabeth's reading level, she got upset and complained that she didn't know most of the words – all of which were just one syllable, such as "did," "car," "say," "rug," and so on. I didn't push it. I felt Elizabeth's pain at not being able to read simple words. I knew that with love and patience, she could become a good reader.

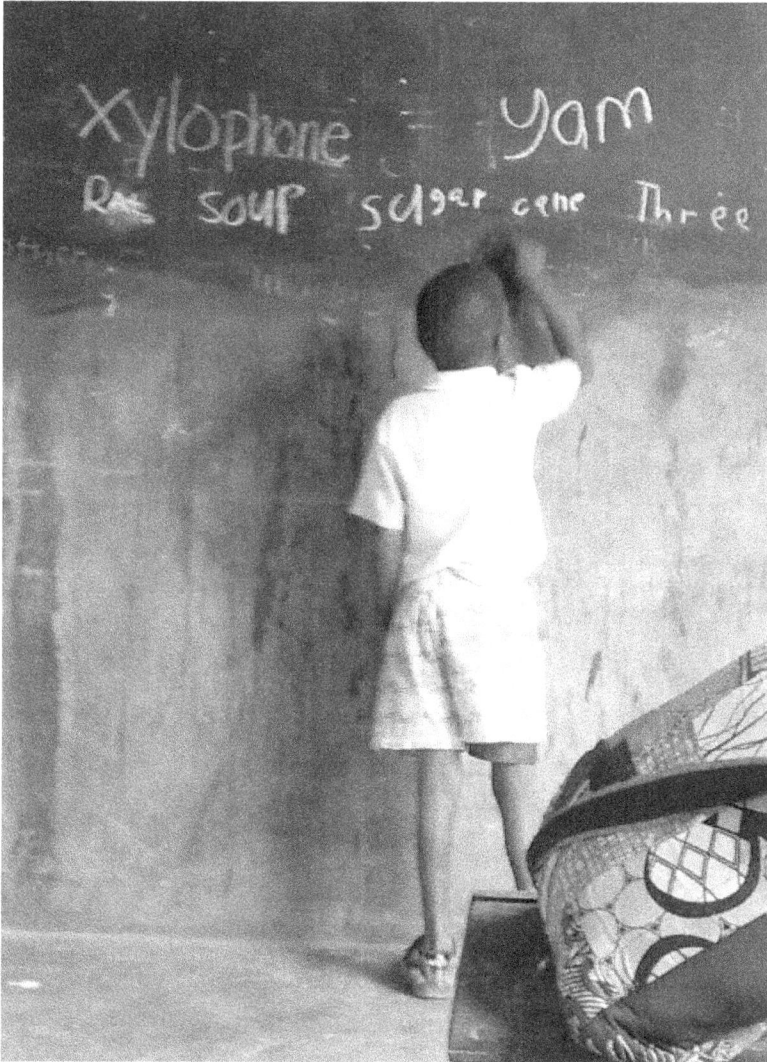

During our first month, Elizabeth was tested by her school and determined to be "borderline mentally retarded" (MR). Some school officials told Elizabeth's mother that she should have her child declared MR so that she could receive more resources.

Elizabeth's mother refused to declare her MR and Elizabeth continued to make gains with me in reading. We began with short stories that I had gotten from a Special Ed teacher for students just learning to read. The stories had monosyllabic words, such as "fish," "shoe," "rock," and "boy." Most stories were just six lines long. After reading the story to and with Elizabeth, I'd ask her to embellish it, for instance, by giving the boy a name, describing the color of his clothing, and naming the street he walked on. Elizabeth was excited by the challenge and because I'd been told that she loved to draw, I invited her to rewrite the story and illustrate it in a short book.

Because Elizabeth had not yet progressed as a reader and writer, I let her dictate the story to me and I wrote it on lined paper. We then made her books out of two folded sheets of construction paper that we stapled on the side. Elizabeth would write her title on the cover, followed by her name as the author and illustrator. The inside page, page 2, might have the date. Pages 3, 4, 5, and 6 contained the story and illustrations, all handwritten by Elizabeth. Page 7 was blank, and page 8 was the back cover. Elizabeth cleverly put ISBN numbers and prices on the back pages. I recall one that she priced at $200! I agreed that her book was at least that valuable for all of the power it contained to change her life as a reader.

Six months after we began working together, Elizabeth had authored at least a dozen books.

She also graduated to reading longer and more complex works.

Early during Elizabeth's 5th grade year, her mother emailed me to say that Elizabeth was having her best year ever. She said my work with Elizabeth during her 4th grade year made her new success in school possible. Elizabeth also emailed. She created a computer-drawn painting and wrote these words: "I love you. I like to read." It's difficult to explain how good it felt to receive that email from Elizabeth and her mom. Her success reassured me that, with love and patience, any child could learn to read.

Here's how you can help young children author and illustrate their own books: Each book you read to and with your child will have a theme. Let's take *Charlie Parker Plays Bebop*. This is a fun book for elementary-aged children that uses words to demonstrate the sounds that the jazz genius Charlie Parker made with his horn. After reading this story, you can have your child think about his favorite instrument and write a book describing some of the sounds the instrument would make. You can follow the same story pattern of the Charlie Parker book. Your child would insert his name and re-title it something like *Kevin Jackson Plays the Bang-Bang Drums*.

To help your child expand his vocabulary while writing the story, encourage him to give his character traits, such as height, hair and eye color, hairstyle, and clothing style. Help him spell words he doesn't know, but don't let him spend too much time trying to spell every word correctly. The goal is to get him to write his own story, about his own character, using his imagination to make it as wild and wonderful as he wants it to be. Editing can come later, as it does for professional writers.

In November 2006, Elizabeth and I read the children's book *What I Do Best*. It was a story about children and the things they did well. One girl took good care of her pets. One boy did his chores well. Another boy was tops in the theater. Another girl was a great artist. Elizabeth is a big fan of a cartoon called *Yin Yang Yo*. She decided to write a book about this character called *Yin Yang Yo Does Karate Best*. It reads in part, "Yin Yang Yo goes to school to learn how to do karate. She practices with her teacher. Her teacher is named Yo. Yin Yang Yo uses karate to fight crime. Yin Yang Yo

fights the evil bug. He is two feet tall and brown. He has purple eyes."

You can see how Elizabeth gave her character a different name, created a setting for her (karate school), and created enemies for her (a brown, two-foot-tall evil bug with purple eyes).

Before creating this story, Elizabeth would not have been able to read many of the words, such as evil, teacher, karate, practices, or crime. But because she created the story out of things she had seen and imagined, she was instantly familiar with the words. And because she created the story, it meant something special to her. She knew she didn't have to fear the bigger words, because they came out of her own mouth. In fact, my definition of writing is talking on paper. I use it whenever a child, including a teenager, tells me they don't know how to write or don't like to write. I let them know that if they can talk, they can write. Interestingly, because Elizabeth loved to talk and draw, I rarely had to encourage her to dictate or write a story. As a result, the more she was able to read and write her own words, the more courage and skill she developed. The very same can happen for your child.

Children, generally, understand words that are more complex than they can read, pronounce, or spell. They also can, and do, use these words in speaking. Once they write the words, they'll have a much easier time reading them. They came from their minds and imaginations; they will never forget what they wrote.

So, what if you have a teenager? Will this remedy work for them? Yes, indeed! Teenagers can write and illustrate books. They also can write short essays, poems, letters to family or friends, book, movie, or music reviews, and songs or raps that could be compiled into a book over several months.

There are tons of online publishing services that will allow you, for a small amount of money, to upload your child's work onto a platform that produces a printed book. This works for books with just text as well as for books with art – although books with art cost more. Still, the costs are reasonable for this one-of-a-kind experience and product, so I highly recommend you publish printed copies of at least one of your children's books or a collection of their writings.

Back to teens: Let them write about any subject that interests them. Professional writers only write what they know and care about because doing so produces the best writing – and it's a whole lot easier to write about what you know and care about. The same is true for young people. Give them permission to write about themselves, their hopes and dreams, their skills, what they dislike, what happens at school, friends, sports, music, movies, other forms of entertainment, religion, books, of course, in response to poetry, magazine articles or comics, inanimate objects such as computers, cameras, cars, clothes, furniture, the environment, favorite places, favorite traditions – let there be no limit. The most important thing is that they talk to the paper.

The book can have a theme, with all essays on sports, travel, or the environment. Or it can be a random collection. Again, just give them permission to talk *aka* write. Because they are not in school, their essays won't be graded and it's not necessary, until you're ready to publish, to check them for grammar or spelling. However, it would be good to keep track of new vocabulary learned in each week's reading (see more on this in the *Make it Fun* chapter) and to encourage your child or teen to use new words in their writing.

I've seen countless teens, who initially had refused to write, put pen to paper.

A summer literacy program at a D.C. high school provides a case in point. We invited students to write essays over five weeks on a variety of subjects and then choose their favorite to publish in a book. I offered more than a dozen topics and also let them choose their own. The most popular topic was *What You Don't Know by Looking at Me*. Ask teens to make a list of things that people wouldn't know about them just by looking at her. They could then turn that list into an essay or poem.

Here's an excerpt from one of the literacy program's teens: "I was born in the summer. I'm the only boy that my mother had. I like to draw like the sun likes to be in the sky. I hate Math like I hate not taking showers..."

And another story. Michael Jackson died during that summer. Ashley was a huge fan. She hadn't written a word until she learned of Michael's death. For the next two weeks, she couldn't stop writing about him and all the memorabilia she had – posters, CDs, magazine articles, and artifacts. Ashley couldn't stop writing because she cared about Michael and she wanted to express the influence he'd had on her – and she did!

We also invited students to write a movie review about the latest comic book character movie. As you might imagine, they had pretty funny ideas about the movie and were eager to share them. We saw little resistance, because, again, giving young people permission to write what they care about makes it easy for them to get in the groove.

Cover of *What You Don't Know by Looking at Me*, a collection of essays by Ballou High School Students, Washington, D.C.

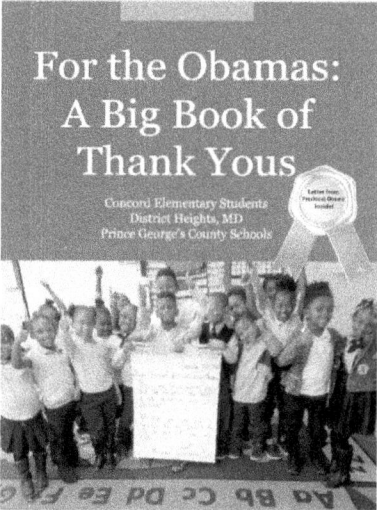

Cover of *For the Obamas: A Big Book of Thank Yous*, a collection of thank you cards and letters by Concord Elementary School

Reading Remedy № 10
Books in Every Case
Make the Library a Wealthy Place

What if the richest woman in America invited your family to her home every year just to hang out? Would you go? Would your heart start beating faster upon walking into her mansion, seeing marble floors, an elegant winding staircase, chandeliers that twinkle like diamonds, and maids and butlers ready to fulfill your every wish? You probably would find it hard to keep from smiling at all the beautiful things that swarm your eyes. You might think that such a fabulous place was just a dream, or that maybe you had died and gone to heaven. When time came for you to go home, you might have a hard time getting into the car. You wouldn't want your dream-like experience to end.

Believe it or not, this is exactly how I feel each time I enter a public library. As beautiful as the homes of Oprah, Bill Gates, Warren Buffett, and other billionaires might be, as far as I'm concerned, they don't compare to the wealth that exists in public libraries. Hear me out. Books can give you level of wealth that you'll never lose – no matter how bad the economy gets, or if the stock market crashes, or housing prices fall to record lows, or if you lose your job, your home, your car, your wife or husband. As I pointed out in the *Why I Read* poem, books can mend a broken heart, turn tears of pain to joy, answer questions for you about your personal life, your professional life, your spiritual life, your mental and physical well-being; books truly enrich your life in ways that are far more meaningful than money alone.

And, because money is important and desirable, you should know that books can help you gain financial wealth too. In fact, it's my sense that most wealthy people spend a lot of time with books – certainly more than they do with television. Reading is key to them attaining wealth, and another good reason for children to improve their skills. A 2011 Georgetown University study called *The College Payoff* showed that people who have at least a bachelor's degree earn a million

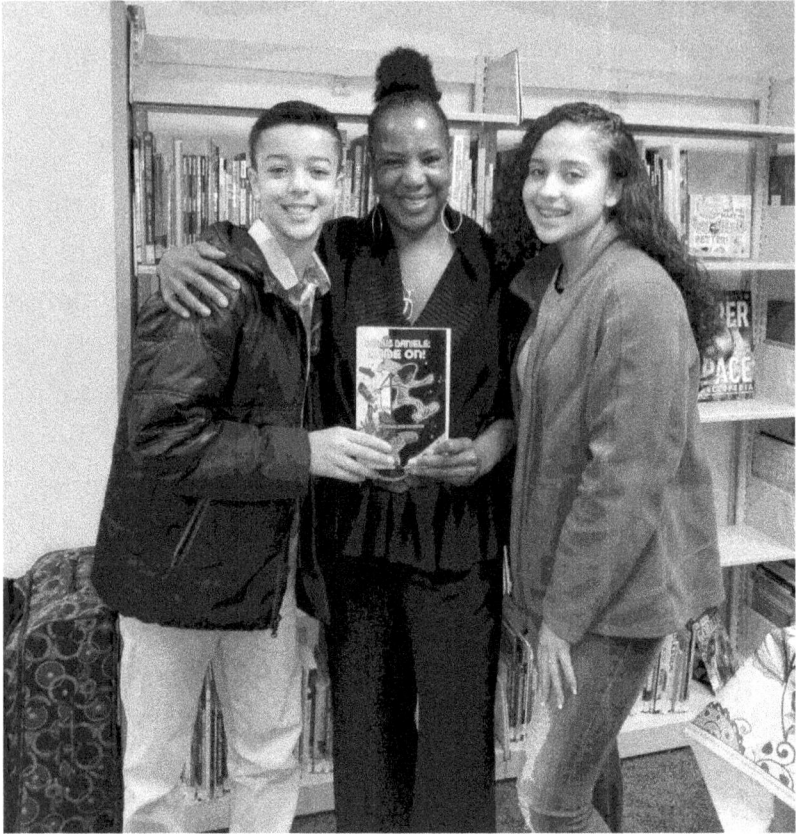

more dollars over their lifetimes than people who stop formal education at high school.

Children need to be good readers to get into college and to graduate. If you start spending more time – at least twice a month – in the library with your children, they are going to become richer with the kinds of knowledge that can inspire self-determination and self-actualization. Regardless of income level, that would seem to be the best outcome.

Reading Remedy Nº· 11

When You Buy Books, the Brighter Your Child's Future Will Look

While you're busy taking your child to the library each week, don't forget to go to some bookstores, including used book bookstores or online stores that

sell used books, at least once a month. Buying books for your children will help them build a home library. Every wealthy and successful person has one.
They love and need books so much that they have to own some.

What's more, new research has shown that having a home library can make a huge difference in a child's reading ability and give children with parents who have not earned a college education a level playing field with children whose parents have attained higher education levels. University of Nevada Researcher Mariah Evans did the 20-year study. According to a Science Daily article in 2010, Evans found that "Both factors, having a 500-book library or having university-educated parents, propel a child 3.2 years further in education, on average."

If you're thinking that a home library might be an expensive thing, think again. Books often cost much less than video games. Before digital music and movies took over, most American homes had large libraries of music CDs and large libraries of DVDs and video games – usually dozens of each kind. While it's nice to have music and movies and games for entertainment, having books is a better investment for children. Books not only provide entertainment, they also, as I mentioned in prior sections, pay you back. Books - more than any educational TV show - will help your children become much better readers and students for the rest of their lives.

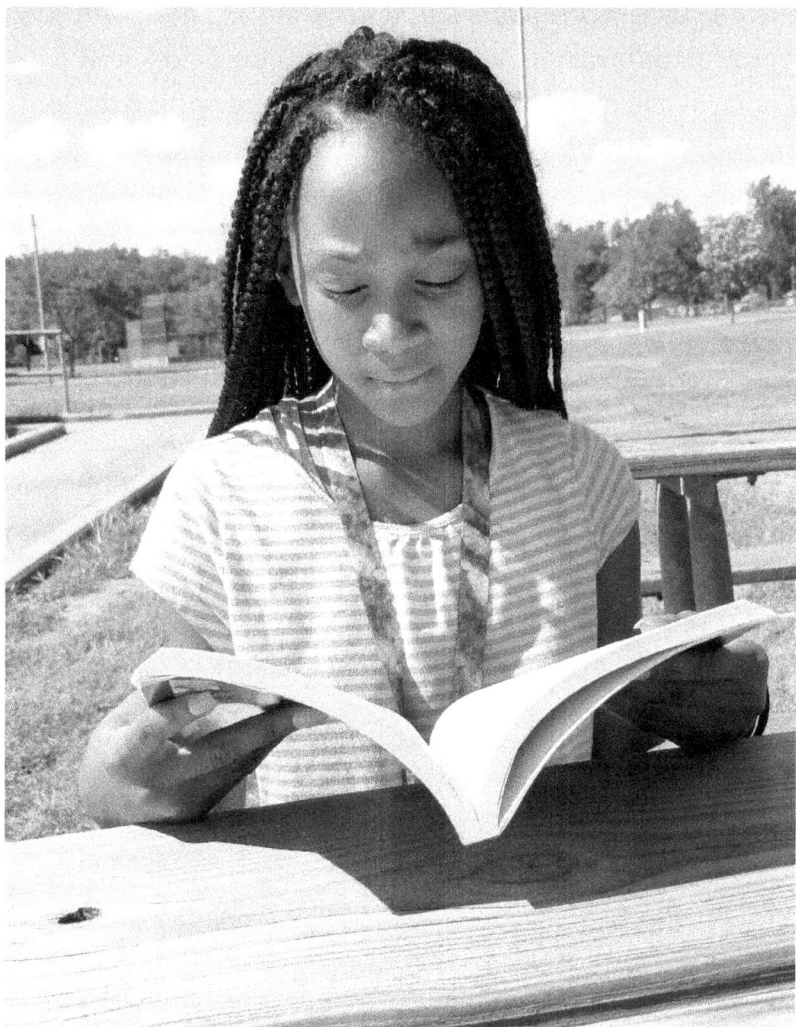

You might wonder what kinds of books you should buy for your children or allow them to bring home. I encourage you to let your children choose – as long as the books don't contain material that's overly violent or sexual and that is not appropriate for their age and maturity level. Children are more likely to read and enjoy books that they pick for themselves.

To start, ask teachers at your child's school, the PTA, your local librarian, local government officials and social service organizations about literacy programs in your community that offer free books. Usually, these programs give free books throughout the year. Also, libraries often partner with literacy programs to give away free books at their locations. In early 2020, I worked with three education programs in Florida that gave away my books to hundreds of children in honor of Martin Luther King Day.

Authors *love* to sell books and they also love to give away books! I have given away thousands upon thousands of books in my life. It's how I met Ivory and became his reading coach. Following authors on social media is a great way to win books during giveaways.

Another way to build your child's library is to encourage relatives and friends who regularly buy gifts for your children to buy them books. Find out your children's favorite authors, genres, and subject matters, and encourage the adults in their lives to make purchases based on what they would enjoy most.

Reading Remedy №· 12

With More Books and Less TV, Children Can Be Whatever They Want to Be

Years ago, I wrote a little song to help children remember the power of books and the problems of TV. The song goes, "If I had a dream, what kind of dream would it be? With more books and less TV, I can be whatever I want to be!"

Except for people in the acting field, you won't find many successful people pointing to spending hours watching TV as the reason for their success. In fact, many actors and filmmakers spend just as much time, if not more, reading.

When my daughters were in middle school, they were pretty much *A* students. However, I noticed that often they would race through their homework so that they could watch their favorite TV shows. It seemed clear that TV was taking up too much of their time. We sat down together and I told them that they could no longer watch TV during the week - only on weekends. They were not pleased. But I didn't just ban TV during the week. I explained why.

I asked them to think about all of their favorite shows and name one show that could help them become a better reader or student. I asked them to name one show that could help them achieve their dreams of going to college and having a career.

They could not name a single show that could do those things for them.

I then explained that while we all enjoy watching TV and movies, we only have so much time each day. While they're in school, they should want to give as much time as possible to getting a good education, because one day that opportunity will be gone. Funny TV shows will still be around, but, if, as children,

they've wasted all their middle and high school years watching TV instead of studying and reading books, they will never get back that time. They'll be playing catch-up for the rest of their lives.

According to an article by the U.S. Department of Education on the Reading is Fundamental site, "Children ages 3 to 5 spend an average of 13 hours and 28 minutes a week watching television...Children under 13 spend 90 minutes a day watching TV... Children of all ages watch as much TV in one day as they read for fun in an entire week."

Without being aware of how little time American children on average were spending watching TV versus reading, my daughters agreed that even though it would be hard, it would be worth it to cut back on TV during the school week. They found more time to read, relax, listen to music, and talk to friends. I even reduced my TV watching and generally only watched shows after they had gone to bed. This gave us the chance to spend more time together. In fact, it wasn't until my oldest daughter was 16 that I bought a TV for their bedroom. Prior to that, we had just one television in the house, and it was in the living room.

I strongly encourage you to enforce the same rules for movies, video and computer games. To keep your children on the reading track, it's also important that you make sure that relatives and friends of your children spend some of their visit reading books, newspapers, magazines, or comics.

It would be wonderful if you could find at least one other parent to join you and your child in creating your own book club.

Children need only one other person to be in their club. Each week they and their friends or relatives could choose a book they want to read from the library. Then, a week later, they could get together to discuss how they felt about the book or the chapters they have read. This is what children naturally do with movies, TV shows, video games, music, and other forms of entertainment.

They text each other, post on Instagram or other social media platforms, call, or meet to talk about what they liked about this song, that musician, this movie, that actor, a new line of clothes or sneakers, or whatever else might excite them at the time.

With all of the enthusiasm that surrounds TV shows, video games, and the latest movies, it's hard for children to choose to read something around friends and family. Your child will need your loving support and leadership to keep reading – especially when everybody else might want to spend hours and hours playing games or watching TV.

Remember, with more books in their lives during the school year, on weekends, holidays and summers, children will have the greatest chance possible to become whatever they hope and dream of being. What greater gift could we, as adults, give a child?

Reading Remedy N⁰· 13
Make it Funky, er, Fun!

Portions of this chapter are excerpted from the author's book *The Happy Teacher and Happy Students*.

James Brown once said on record, "Whatever you do, it's got to be funky." I say, if you want a *superstar* reader, whatever you do, you've got to make reading fun! You must include recreation – refreshment in body and mind – every day in every way imaginable.

I have often had the distinct pleasure of being told by students that my readings or workshops were "fun." And children have added, "and I didn't even have to learn anything." That's what a little bit of fun will do for some children – make them totally unaware that they, indeed, are learning.

Some of the easiest ways to make reading and learning to read fun have already been discussed throughout this book – reading fun books, reading with excitement and drama, reading rhyming books, and using repetition.

Here are more ideas. I often begin reading time with dances and exercise. Really. I do. I know that children will be sitting for 30 minutes or more and will have to concentrate fiercely on what's being read. Giving them the opportunity to dance before, during, or after reading is a terrific way to keep them motivated. They think it's fun and it can also calm them, center them, and get those neurons firing.

Another important way to make reading more enjoyable is to lead children in deep breathing. Take about five deep circular breaths, breathing in through the nose and out through the mouth. Children who are learning to read or who have trouble reading often get nervous and tense when they have to read in front of or with someone, even if that someone is a loving adult. Making it a practice to take deep breaths before reading will help the child release tension and relax.

Physical exercise also helps young children and children with short attention spans release pent-up energy. Once they do, they are more likely to sit down and keep their focus on reading. A one-to-two-minute break should be good enough. Children new to reading

on a daily basis might have trouble keeping still in the beginning. But the more practice they get reading in a loving and patient environment, the more they will get used to reading and won't have as much trouble sitting still.

Reading is one of the best workouts you can ever give the brain. Scientists now know that we have the power to re-wire our brains. We can train our brains to work harder and smarter for us. Keeping the blood flowing to the brain through deep breathing, exercise, and dancing helps it work better and for longer periods of time. It also helps it to grow stronger. And most children love getting up and moving.

And then there are games! Children – and adults – enjoy games. Games are the "secret sauce" to boost learning of all kinds. Reading is no exception.

Renowned Teacher and Author Louanne Johnson recommends *The Big Book of Games* for finding great brain teasers, puzzles, and word games that can be adapted to any subject. I also found *Games for Reading* by Peggy Kaye to contain a bunch of helpful resources. She mentions having fun while reading packaging materials, recipes, making scrapbooks, and children's magazines. I would add that engaging children in writing postcards and letters to close family and friends and developing stories about their own personal history or the family's history are other fun and easy ways to experience reading and writing while improving those skills.

Remember Chapter 6, *Ask to Find Out What the Book's About?* When you craft "closed" questions to ask children as they read, keep them handy in a notebook so that after the story you can play your own version of *Jeopardy!*. It could work like this: If it's just you and one child, draw 12 squares with four columns and three rows. Come up with four simple topics from the story, such as places, characters, numbers, and teams. Write a question on three squares under each topic and give it a dollar value. For instance, one question under Places could be, "In what town was Jeremy born?" Another might be, "Where did the Nelson family go on vacation?" Put each question face down in its group and mix them up. Then line them up in the column. You and your child will randomly choose questions. Each correct answer results in that player getting that much money added to his account. It might

be easier to take turns answering questions (unlike in *Jeopardy!* where you can only choose a question if you answer the preceding one correctly.) Play until all questions are answered. The player with the biggest bank account wins.

You can add more columns or topics and questions if you have more players or if you want to increase the challenge for your child. My favorite reading/literacy game, however, is Vocabulary "BINGO." It took several hours for me to create 25 different "BINGO" cards based on words from an autobiography that had dozens of medical terms – including words that I didn't know how to define. But the 5th graders, most of whom were below grade level in reading, were completely engaged and attuned to the process of calling out the words and their definitions. It was clear they enjoyed the game and learned from it.

Calling out the words over and over again reminded students of how they were pronounced. It gave them the opportunity to become better acquainted with how the words were spelled. And I used the opportunity to remind the students of the definitions.

After an hour of play, not a single student was ready to quit, and undoubtedly quite a few didn't realize how much they were learning.

If it's just you and one or two children, you can create "BINGO" cards together in about 30 minutes.

You might be wondering where to get the vocabulary words to play Vocabulary "BINGO." Glad you asked! As you read with your child, keep a notebook handy to write down words she stumbles over or doesn't know the meaning of. Let her know that the reason you're keeping the list is so that she can master those words, including by playing Vocabulary "BINGO." During the reading, ask her to repeat three times any word that she finds difficult to pronounce or doesn't know the meaning of. After each day's reading session, ask her to reread the words to see if she remembers how to pronounce them. Add all the words each week to a Superstar Vocabulary Word chart, so that from week to week she can see how many more words she has added to her vocabulary! You could use plain white paper or construction paper to make this chart and tape each new set of words on a prominent wall, such as her bedroom wall. If she learns 10 new words each week, after 12 weeks, her Superstar Vocabulary Word chart would have 120 words! That should make her feel great and it gives her a visible sign of her progress and success.

You've also got a long list of words to use to play Vocabulary "BINGO." Instructions to create your game card are at the end. Elizabeth, the fourth grader I tutored for some of the 2006-2007 school year, fell head over hills in love with Vocabulary "BINGO" and wanted to play every time I visited. It was a new and exciting way for her to get more acquainted with words.

Vocabulary "BINGO" felt to Elizabeth more like play than "learning," which for her had always been difficult and painful. I added some extra fun to our game by making pennies our "BINGO" chips. You also could use M&M's candies as chips.

These "BINGO" games were also a big hit with the Special Education middle-schoolers who told me (almost angrily) they wanted to play more rather than learn academics. Instead of being upset, their thirst for more games motivated me. I created "BINGO" cards based on rhyming words, proper nouns, historical figures and places, and themes from reading materials we used.

The Friday before Christmas break that school year, Joshua joined the teacher and me as we led the students in Vocabulary "BINGO" using words from a short book the children had read on the pyramids of

Egypt. The teacher gave a Reese's Cup to each student who got "BINGO," and I gave each winner a quarter. We had six students. I'd forgotten to get the colorfully decorated pencils that I normally buy for prizes, so I used quarters.

Before we began playing, I told the students that I was proud of them for coming to school on a day when few of their classmates and friends showed up. (Fourteen students were assigned to the class). I gave them a little speech that likened coming to school to investing in themselves. I told them that with each day in school, they're learning and growing and eventually would be able to earn money at the kind of job or career they wanted.

When they come to school, I emphasized, it's as if they're building up a bank account. I told them their teacher and I would give them a surprise at the end of class.

The teacher and I awarded each student $1.00 as a surprise. They were all ecstatic. Some jumped up and down as if they'd won the lottery. It was something to see. I knew they'd enjoy getting the dollar, but I didn't expect to see that kind of joy. Then I turned to look at the boy who had started the school year with an unbelievably foul mouth but had calmed and buckled down in recent weeks. He had won the most "BINGO" games and was going home with $1.75 and three Reese's Cups. He wasn't bouncing around like his classmates. He sat quietly, looked up, and then as a wide grin spread across his face solemnly declared, "This is the happiest day of my life."

The teacher, Joshua, and I were amazed. It was another misty-eyed moment for me. All children want so badly to WIN at something in life, to feel good about themselves, to feel capable. A small thing such as winning some quarters and candy seems to have gone a long way towards giving them the sense that maybe, just maybe, they could be winners. Maybe they could be Reading Superstars!

Of course, to keep these students motivated, the opportunities to win have to show up repeatedly, and as often, if not more often, than those opportunities to lose. And it's we, as parents, guardians, youth workers, and family friends who constantly have to provide the opportunities for them. That's what this book is all about. I share this story only to emphasize how a little recreation can go a long way toward building great relationships with children – and make a major impact on their desire to learn.

As Johnson put it, "...No matter how old they act, children are still children, and they need to laugh, to play, to create, to stretch their imaginations, and tickle their brains...Laughter heals the body, soothes the soul, and stimulates the brain. It also makes a long school day (or challenging and fear-inducing learning experience) much more enjoyable."

That goes for us as adults. Recreation is not just about playing, although in a learning setting, playing

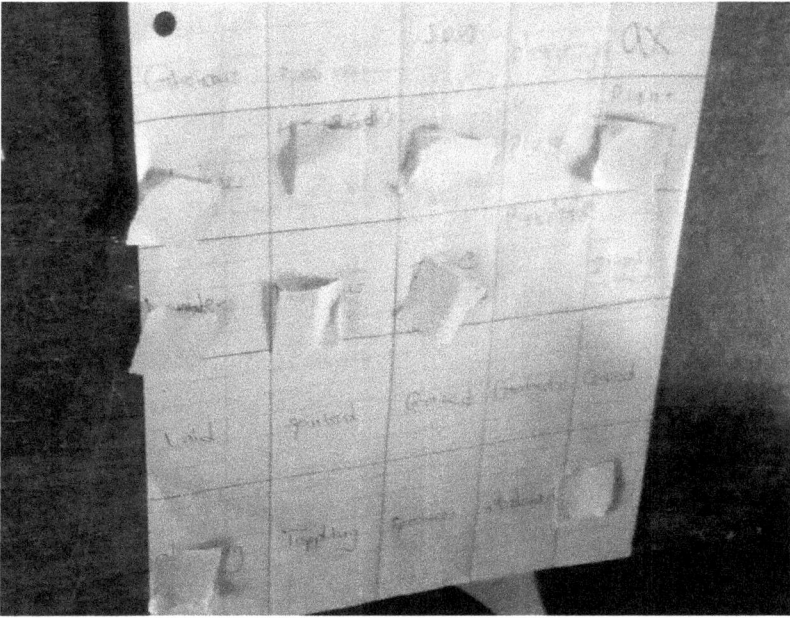

ought to be allowed and encouraged. Recreation, indeed, is also about healing. If our children and we as parents and community members need anything, we need healing. It is my fervent hope that *Parent Power: How to Raise a Reading Superstar* can be a potent source.

One last comment on making reading fun. Create a bookworm chart, in the same way you create the Superstar Vocabulary Word chart, on plain white or construction paper. For the bookworm chart, however, include three rows. One row for the name of each book. Another row for the number of books your child reads. The final row for the number of pages your child reads in each book.

That way, when your child reads longer books, he'll feel proud of his progress tackling so many more pages. I look forward to hearing about the great successes that you and the children in your life experience in the months and years to come.

How to Play Vocabulary "BINGO"

On an 8.5 x 11 sheet of blank paper, draw 25 squares, including a Free Space in the center.

You can also go to www.carolinebrewerbooks.com to download a blank card that can be printed out.

Obama	mama	kid	bid	cope
hope	frogs	dogs	hogs	sent
president	go	**PARENT POWER**	care	everywhere
sent	know	sun	agreed	proceed
creed	sow	run	day	say

From *Barack Obama: A Hip Hop Tale* Vocabulary Rhyming Cards ©2008

Create a list of at least 30 words. Each word from your vocabulary list should be written on separate index cards or small squares of paper and those cards should be placed in a container.

Each player should review the master list to find the 24 words she wants to write on her game card.

After game cards are made, begin the game by drawing the index cards from the container and announcing them one at a time.

Give players a chance to locate the term on their cards. Use plastic chips, pennies, M&Ms®, or small paper squares as chips.

A winning card will have five items in a row - across, down, or diagonally - (including free space) covered. The winner should announce, "I got _Vocabulary BINGO!_"

Play until you're satisfied.

About the Author

Caroline Brewer is more than an author and education consultant. She is a literacy activist. She motivates children and teens to read (and write) by dissolving their fears; fears that they will struggle, fail, be humiliated, bored, unable to identify with or understand book characters or themes or write with meaning.

She introduces written material and writing opportunities to youth in a highly engaging, strategic, and compassionate way that aids them in conquering anxieties and apathy.

Her approach also helps teachers, parents, and tutors gain the skills and confidence to inspire literacy success. Ultimately, children uncover the joy and possibilities of reading and self-expression.

Caroline has consulted and presented readings, speeches, and seminars in seven states, D.C., and Ghana, West Africa to 25,000 teachers, children, tutors, parents, and librarians.

Caroline has a background as an award-winning journalist and served on two Pulitzer Prize juries. Her work was nominated for The Pulitzer Prize.

She is the author of 12 books, mother of two, and lives in Washington, D.C.

Go to www.carolinebrewerbooks.com
or email caroline@carolinebrewerbooks.com
to bring **Caroline Brewer as a Speaker** or the
Parent Power Training Experience to your organization!

Bring the **Parent Power Experience** to your school, library, PTA program, youth organization, or church and watch a garden of great readers and achievers grow!

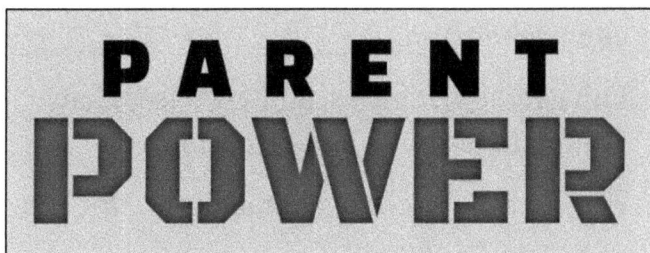

PARENT POWER

EXPERIENCE

Parent Power: How to Raise a Reading Superstar is an excellent book and it's also a fun, highly engaging, and interactive *experience*, created by Education Consultant and Children's Book Author Caroline Brewer. Participants get to dance, sing, clap, and play instruments – not to mention read – all for the cause of making reading come alive for children, teens, and adults.

Participants in the **Parent Power Experience** will learn:

- The first and most important way that children learn;

- The fastest way to increase reading ability;

- How to close the multi-million word gap with wealthy children;

- How to nurture improvement in just minutes a day;

- How children/teens can give them the secrets to motivating them to read;

- The tricks medical students use to boost comprehension;

- Fun games, activities, and exercises that stimulate learning and retention;

- How to build a child's home library for free or very little money.

Whether a child is diagnosed with a learning disability, emotional disability, is taking medication, hasn't warmed up to books or is hostile to them, is a toddler or teen, **Parent Power** provides keys to a reading revolution.

Go to www.carolinebrewerbooks.com or email caroline@carolinebrewerbooks.com to bring on the Parent Power Training Experience!

www.ingramcontent.com/pod-product-compliance
Lightning Source LLC
Chambersburg PA
CBHW072205090426
42740CB00012B/2401